TABLE TRAIL 1

Date:

Fill in the empty frames

			3				4				10
							8				
2		6	8		14		18			
		9								25
					20					
		15								40
					28					
		21								
		27			40					

Finish these by drawing arrows.

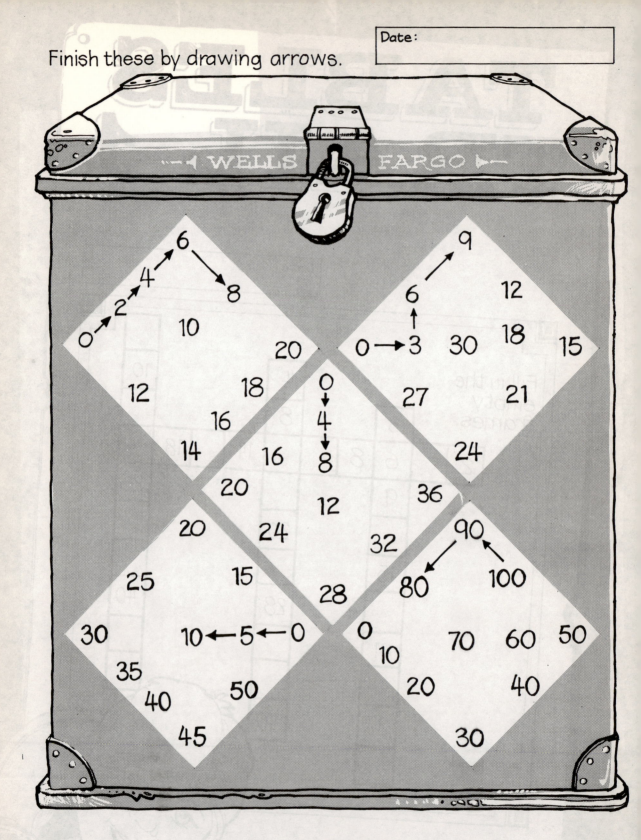

Finish these by putting the correct numbers in the empty frames.

Date:

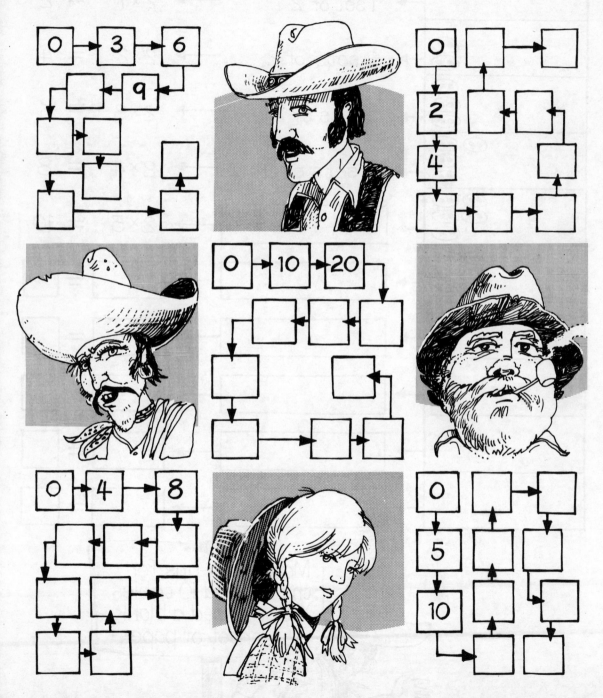

Finish this build-up of the 2 table.

Date:

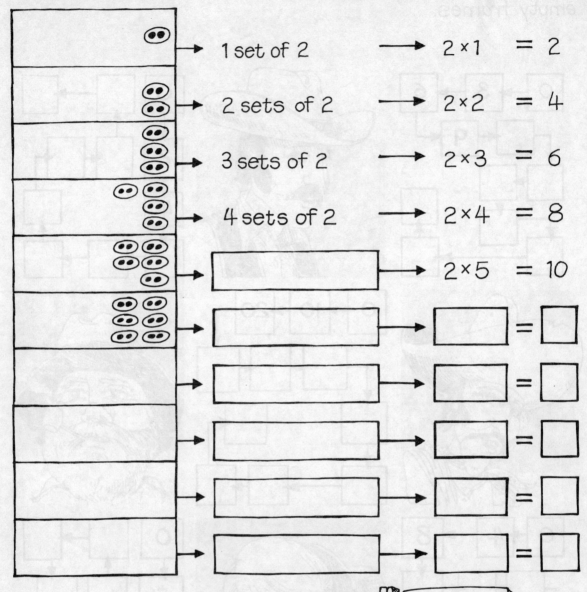

1 set of 2 → 2 × 1 = 2

2 sets of 2 → 2 × 2 = 4

3 sets of 2 → 2 × 3 = 6

4 sets of 2 → 2 × 4 = 8

2 × 5 = 10

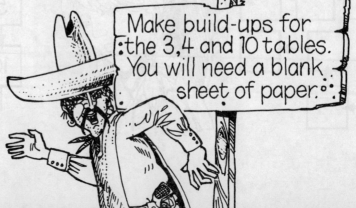

Make build-ups for the 3, 4 and 10 tables. You will need a blank sheet of paper.

Complete this build-up of the 3 table.

3 ▶	3	3×1
6 ▶	3+3	3×2
9 ▶	3+3+3	3×3
12 ▶	3+3+3+3	
15 ▶		
18 ▶		
21 ▶		
24 ▶		
27 ▶		
30 ▶		

Complete this build-up of the 5 table.

5 ▶	5	5×1
10 ▶	5+5	5×2
15 ▶	5+5+5	
20 ▶	5+5+5+5	
25 ▶		
30 ▶		
35 ▶		
40 ▶		
45 ▶		
50 ▶		

Write build-ups for the 4 and 10 tables. You will need a blank sheet of paper.

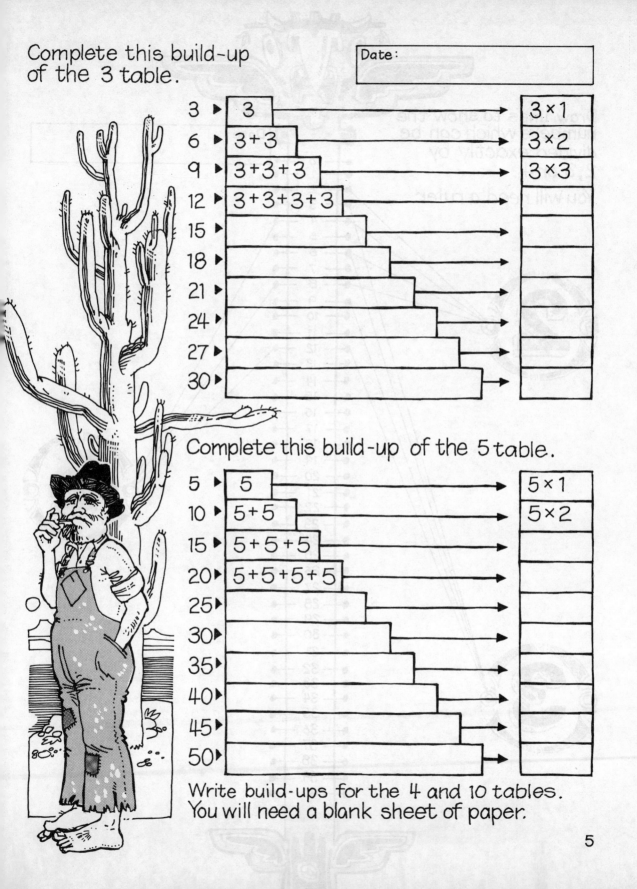

5

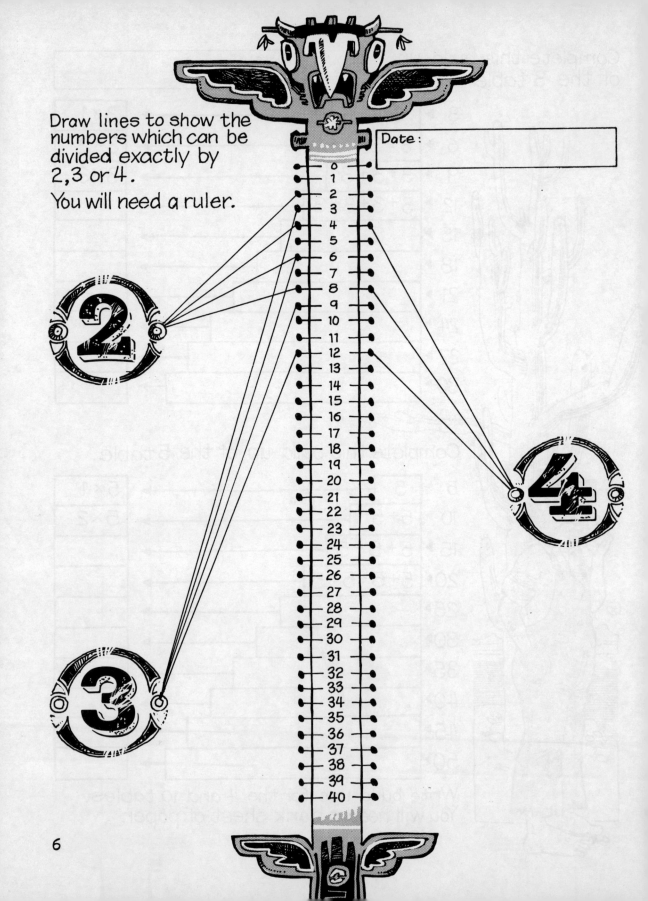

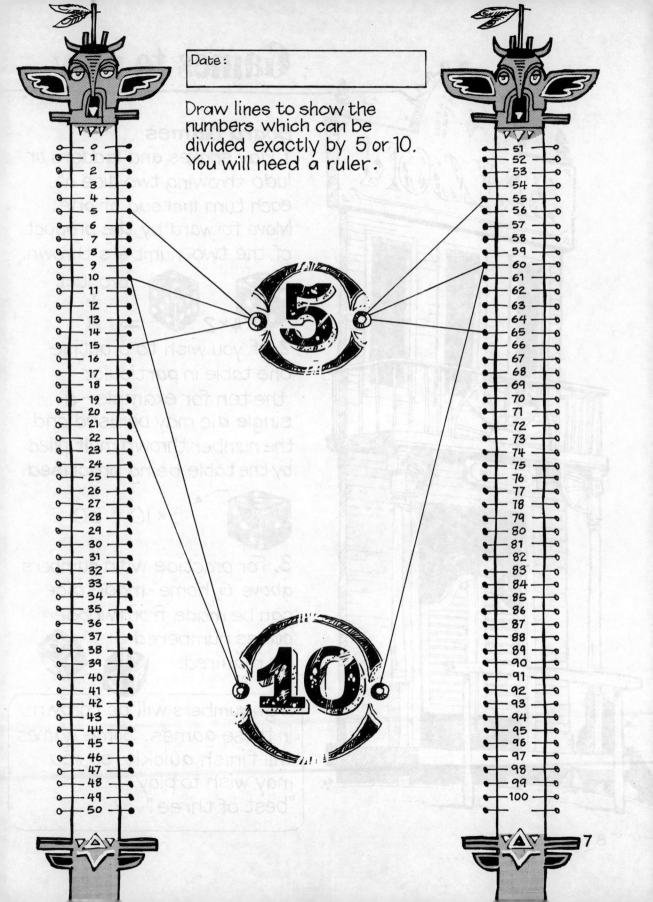

Games to play

Board Games

1. Play snakes and ladders or ludo throwing two dice at each turn instead of one. Move forward by the product of the two numbers thrown.

4 × 2 = product → 8

2. If you wish to practise one table in particular — the ten for example — a single die may be used and the number thrown multiplied by the table being practised.

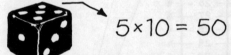

5 × 10 = 50

3. For practice with numbers above 6, home-made dice can be made from wooden cubes numbered as required.

High numbers will be thrown in these games. Some games will finish quickly, so you may wish to play "best of three."

Ask for help with these games.
You will need some friends.

Tables Cards

The cards may be cut from cardboard of any convenient size. You will need to make 100 cards. Each card should be marked with a tables question (or factors) on one side $\boxed{3 \times 4 =}$ and the answer (or product) on the reverse $\boxed{12}$ Make a card for each tables fact up to $\boxed{10 \times 10}$.

1. Three or more players

One player holds the cards and shows the side marked with the factors $\boxed{7 \times 5}$ to the other players. The first to call the correct product wins the card. The game ends when all the cards have been used and the player with most cards is the winner.

2. Play as above but show the product side of the card $\boxed{20}$. The first to give a correct pair of factors wins the card.

Note — There will be a number of correct answers for some products.

$\boxed{20} \rightarrow \boxed{10 \times 2} \boxed{4 \times 5}$
$ \boxed{2 \times 10} \boxed{5 \times 4}$

3. Two players

The cards are shared equally between the players who take turns in showing a card and answering. A correct answer wins the card. Player with most cards at the end is the winner.

Note — Factor or product side of cards may be used.

9

100 Square

Date:

Colour all the numbers which can be divided exactly by 2.
These are called $\boxed{e\_\_\_}$ numbers.

1	2	✗	4	5	✗	7	8	✗	10
11	12	13	14	15	16	17	18	19	20
21	22	23	24	25	26	27	28	29	30
31	32	33	34	35	36	37	38	39	40
41	42	43	44	45	46	47	48	49	50
51	52	53	54	55	56	57	58	59	60
61	62	63	64	65	66	67	68	69	70
71	72	73	74	75	76	77	78	79	80
81	82	83	84	85	86	87	88	89	90
91	92	93	94	95	96	97	98	99	100

Now put a cross on each number which can be divided exactly by 3.

Write all the numbers which can be divided exactly by 2 and by 3.

☐ ☐ ☐ ☐ ☐ ☐ ☐ ☐ ☐ ☐ ☐ ☐ ☐ ☐

Finish these:

Date:

×2
- 2 → 4
- 3 → 6
- 5 → 10
- 6 →
- 7 →
- 1 →
- 4 →
- 9 →
- 10 →
- 8 →

×3
- 2 → 6
- 3 → 9
- 4 →
- 6 →
- 5 →
- 1 →
- 10 →
- 7 →
- 9 →
- 8 →

×10
- 3 → 30
- 2 →
- 5 →
- 4 →
- 7 →
- 6 →
- 9 →
- 8 →
- 1 →
- 10 →

×4
- 10 →
- 1 →
- 2 →
- 5 →
- 4 →
- 3 →
- 6 →
- 8 →
- 9 →
- 7 →

×5
- 2 →
- 9 →
- 4 →
- 7 →
- 6 →
- 5 →
- 8 →
- 3 →
- 10 →
- 1 →

Dot patterns

Date:

This may be recorded as
3 × 5 (five lots of three)
or
5 × 3 (three lots of five)

Record these dot patterns in two ways.

Draw dot patterns for

5 × 5

3 × 8

4 × 7

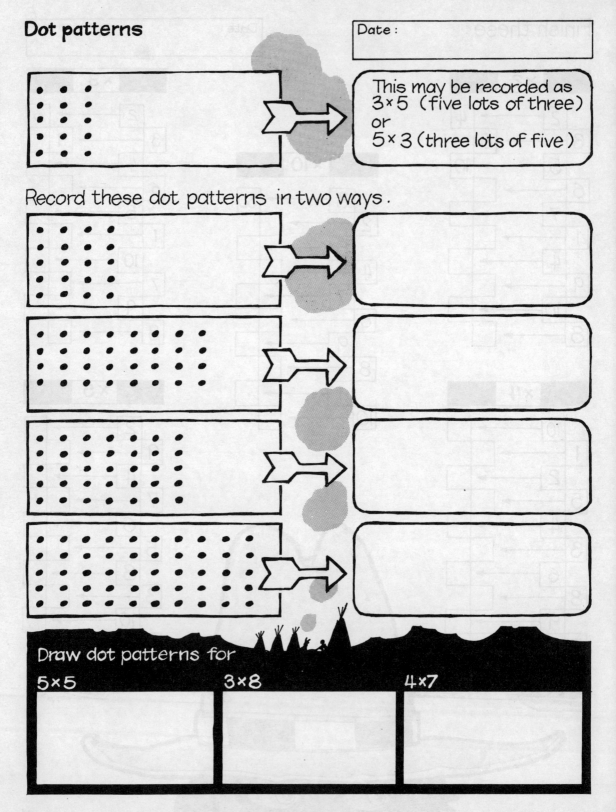

Complete these: Date:

2 × 4 = 4 × 2
3 × 2 = ☐ × 3
5 × 2 = 2 × ☐
6 × 3 = ☐ × 6
2 × ☐ = 6 × ☐
☐ × 3 = 7 × ☐
8 × 3 = 3 × ☐
8 × 2 = ☐ × 8
9 × ☐ = 3 × ☐
10 × 2 = ☐ × ☐
3 × ☐ = 10 × ☐

2 × 5 = 5 × 2
4 × 4 = ☐ × 4
5 × 3 = 3 × ☐
5 × 6 = 6 × ☐
5 × 5 = ☐ × ☐
7 × 5 = ☐ × ☐
7 × 4 = ☐ × 7
8 × ☐ = 4 × 8
5 × ☐ = 8 × ☐
9 × ☐ = ☐ × 4
9 × 3 = ☐ × ☐

10 × 0 ⟶ 0 ⟵ 0 × 10
10 × 1 ⟶ 10 ⟵ 1 × ☐
10 × 2 ⟶ 20 ⟵ ☐ × ☐
☐ × 3 ⟶ 30 ⟵ 3 × ☐
10 × ☐ ⟶ 40 ⟵ ☐ × 10
10 × ☐ ⟶ 50 ⟵ ☐ × 10
☐ × 6 ⟶ 60 ⟵ 6 × ☐
☐ × 7 ⟶ 70 ⟵ ☐ × ☐
☐ × ☐ ⟶ 80 ⟵ ☐ × ☐
☐ × ☐ ⟶ 90 ⟵ ☐ × ☐
☐ × ☐ ⟶ 100 ⟵ ☐ × ☐

True or false. Write whether these are true or false and make the false statements true.

Date:

BAR X RANCH

2 × 2 = 4	true	✓
3 × 2 = 5	false	3 × 2 = 6
4 × 4 = 16	true	✓
5 × 3 = 15		
2 × 7 = 15		
8 × 3 = 22		
10 × 4 = 40		
5 × 7 = 34		
5 × 9 = 45		
9 × 5 = 46		
8 × 4 = 32		
8 × 3 = 29		
7 × 4 = 28		
7 × 3 = 20		
6 × 7 = 44		
4 × 0 = 1		
4 × 1 = 4		
3 × 0 = 0		
10 × 1 = 0		

Complete these multiplication frames.

Date:

×	2	4	6	8	10
2	4	8			
4			24		
3					
5				40	
10					

×	3	2	6	5	4
2					
5			30		
4					
3					
10					

×	4	6	7	10	8
4					
3					
5					
2				20	
10					

×	5	6	9	8	7
2					
5			45		
3					
10					
4					

Now try to complete this frame →

×	3	2							
4	12	8		20		28	40		36
2			8						18
3	9	6		15		21		24	
10			40		60				
5					30		50	40	

15

100 Square

Date:

1. Place a cross in the top left hand corner of each number which can be divided exactly by 5 → $\boxed{\overset{\times}{5}}$

1	2	3	4	×5	6	7	8	9	×10△
11	12	13	14	×15	16	17	18	19	×20△
21	22	23	24	25	26	27	28	29	30
31	32	33	34	35	36	37	38	39	40
41	42	43	44	45	46	47	48	49	50
51	52	53	54	55	56	57	58	59	60
61	62	63	64	65	66	67	68	69	70
71	72	73	74	75	76	77	78	79	80
81	82	83	84	85	86	87	88	89	90
91	92	93	94	95	96	97	98	99	100

2. Place a triangle in the top right hand corner of each number which can be divided by 10. $\boxed{10^{\triangle}}$

3. Draw a circle in the bottom left hand corner of each number which can be divided by 4. $\boxed{\underset{\circ}{8}}$

4. Draw a square in the bottom right hand corner of each number which can be divided by 3. $\boxed{9_{\square}}$

16

TABLES TRAIL 2

Date:

Fill in the empty frames.

				9			
	8						
	16			27			
6		18		30		42		54	
	32			45			
	48			63			
	64			81			
	80						

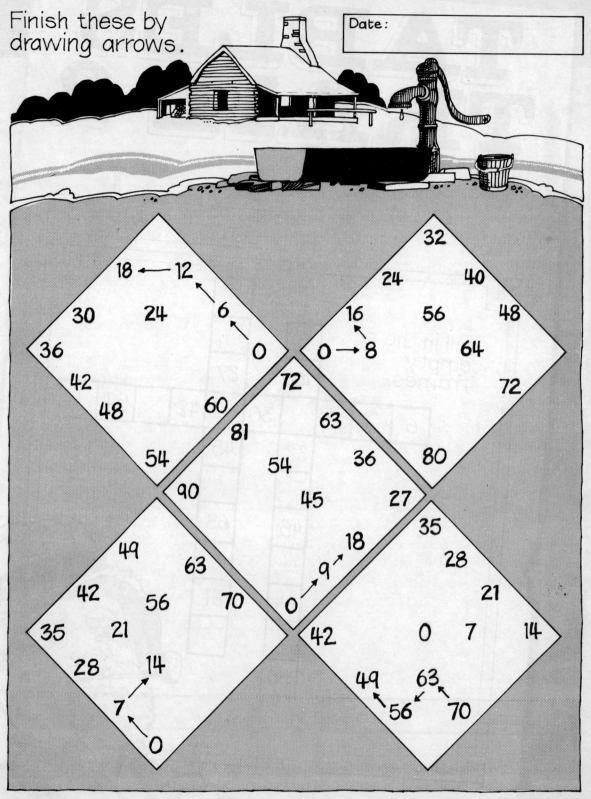
Finish these by drawing arrows.

Finish this build-up of the 7 table.

Date:

→ 1 set of 7 → 7×1 = 7

→ 2 sets of 7 → 7×2 = 14

→ 3 sets of 7 → ☐ = ☐

→ 4 sets of 7 → ☐ = ☐

→ ☐ → ☐ = ☐

→ ☐ → ☐ = ☐

→ 7 sets of 7 → ☐ = ☐

→ ☐ → ☐ = ☐

→ ☐ → ☐ = ☐

→ ☐ → ☐ = ☐

Make build-ups for the 6, 8 and 9 tables. You will need a blank sheet of paper.

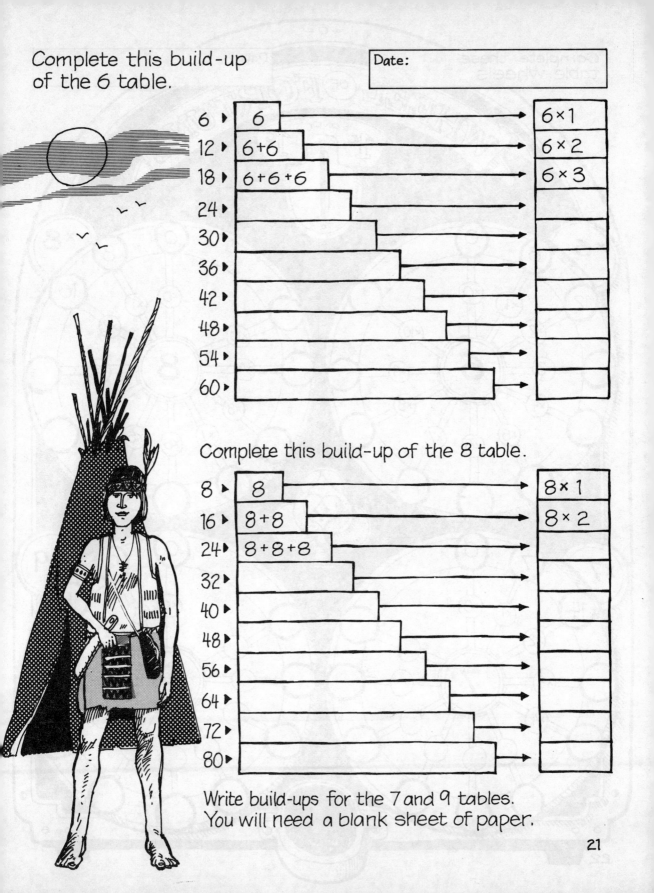

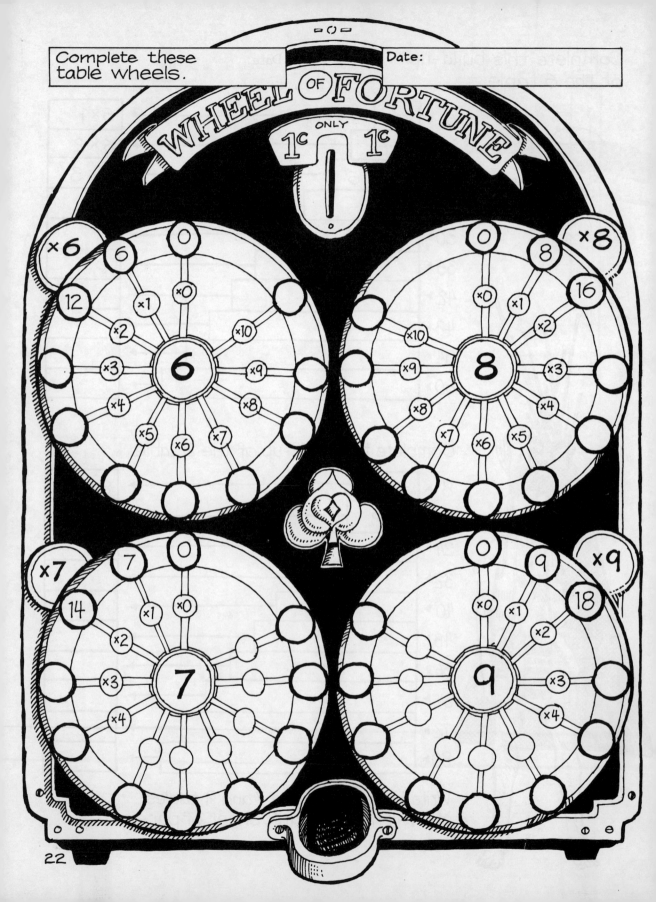

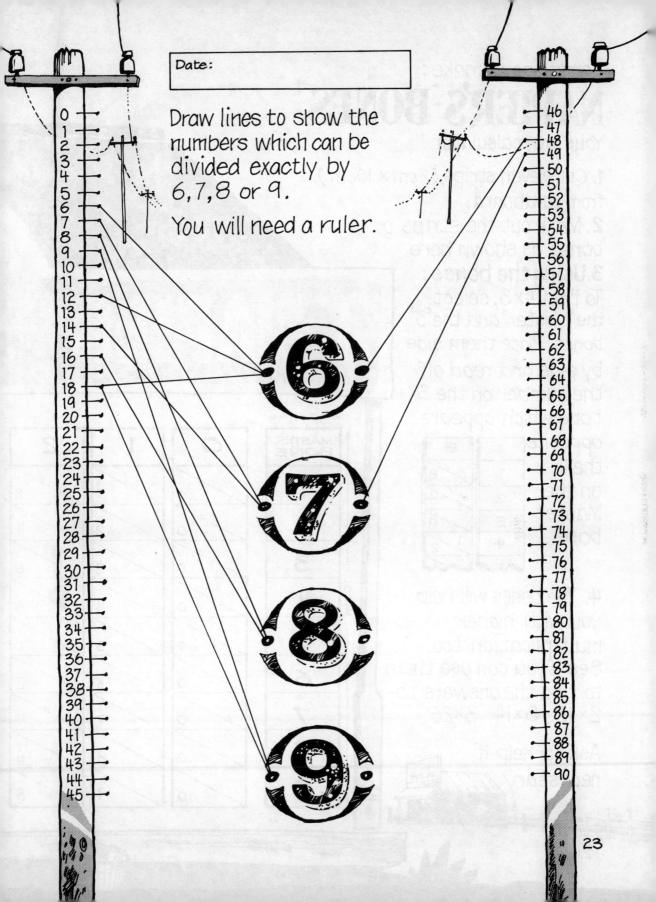

Something to make:
NAPIER'S BONES*
Your own calculator!

1. Cut eleven strips, (2cm × 10cm), from cardboard.

2. Mark out the strips or 'bones' as shown here.

3. Using the bones:
To find 4×3, select the 'Master' and the '3' bones. Place them side by side and read off the number on the 3 bone which appears opposite the 4 on the Master bone.

4. The bones will help you with higher multiplication too. See if you can use them to find the answers to—
2×12   5×14   3×26

Ask for help if necessary.

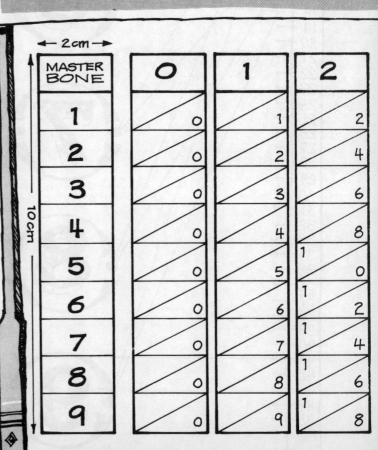

✱ This simple device for helping with multiplication was invented by John Napier, a Scottish mathematician, in the 17th century. The strips were originally carved in bone.

GENERAL STORE & TRADING POST

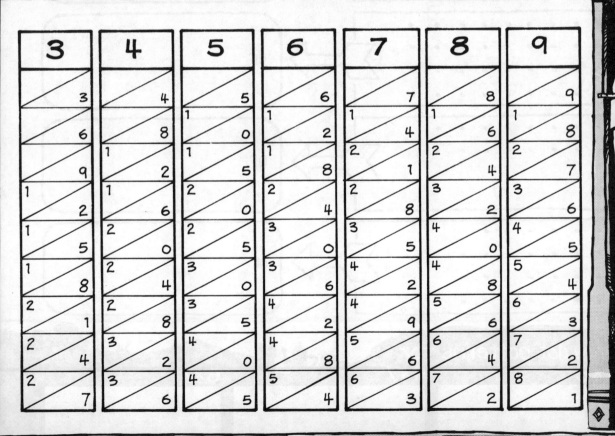

Dot patterns.

Date:

This may be recorded as
6 × 3 (three lots of six) or
3 × 6 (six lots of three).

Record these dot patterns in two ways.

7 × 2 (two lots of seven)
or

4 × 5 (five lots of four)
or

or

or

or

Draw dot patterns for
7 × 8   9 × 7   6 × 7

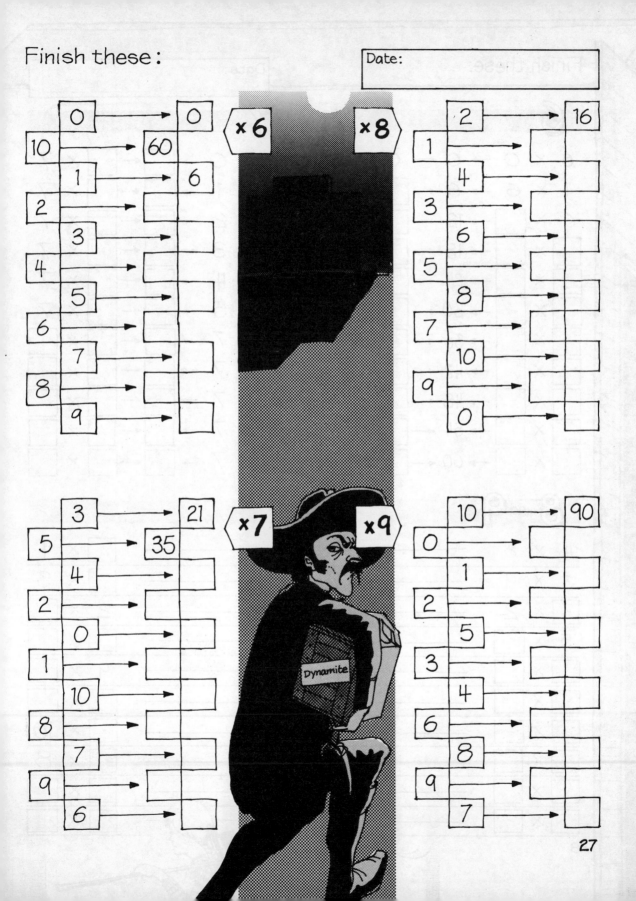

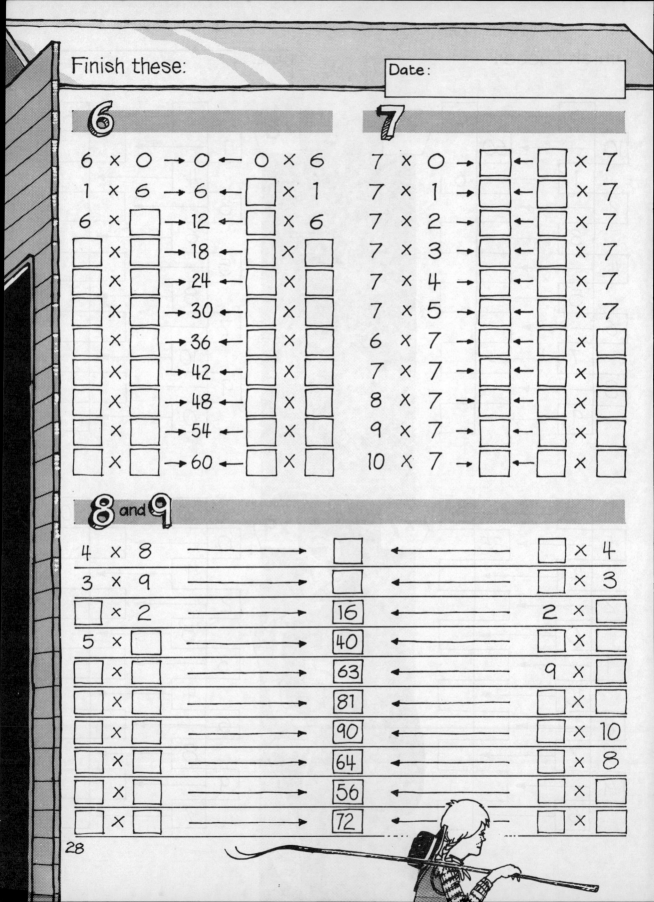

True or false. Write whether these are true or false and make the false statements true.

5 × 6 = 30	true	✓
7 × 6 = 40	false	7 × 6 = 42
6 × 3 = 20		
9 × 6 = 54		
10 × 7 = 70		
7 × 7 = 50		
7 × 4 = 30		
7 × 9 = 62		
2 × 8 = 16		
8 × 5 = 40		
8 × 7 = 57		
9 × 4 = 36		
10 × 8 = 105		
8 × 9 = 3		
9 × 7 = 63		

Dividing and multiplying are connected. Complete these:

Date:

6 × 5 = 30 ⟶ 30 ÷ 5 = 6 ⟶ 30 ÷ 6 = 5
6 × 4 = ☐ ⟶ ☐ ÷ 4 = 6 ⟶ ☐ ÷ 6 = ☐
6 × 7 = ☐ ⟶ ☐ ÷ 6 = ☐ ⟶ ☐ ÷ ☐ = 6
6 × ☐ = 60 ⟶ 60 ÷ ☐ = 10 ⟶ 60 ÷ 10 = ☐

8 × 3 = ☐ ⟶ 24 ÷ 3 = ☐ ⟶ ☐ ÷ ☐ = 3
☐ × 6 = 48 ⟶ 48 ÷ 6 = ☐ ⟶ 48 ÷ ☐ = 6
9 × 8 = ☐ ⟶ ☐ ÷ 9 = ☐ ⟶ ☐ ÷ ☐ = 9
☐ × ☐ = 64 ⟶ 64 ÷ ☐ = ☐ ⟶ 64 ÷ ☐ = ☐

7 × ☐ = 56 ⟶ 56 ÷ 7 = ☐ ⟶ 56 ÷ 8 = ☐
9 × ☐ = 63 ⟶ ☐ ÷ 9 = ☐ ⟶ 63 ÷ ☐ = 9
10 × ☐ = 70 ⟶ 70 ÷ 7 = ☐ ⟶ 70 ÷ ☐ = 7
☐ × ☐ = 42 ⟶ 42 ÷ 7 = ☐ ⟶ ☐ ÷ 6 = 7

Make up your own examples for the 9 table.

9 × 4 = ☐ ⟶ ☐ ÷ ☐ = ☐ ⟶ ☐ ÷ ☐ = ☐
9 × 7 = ☐ ⟶ ☐ ÷ ☐ = ☐ ⟶ ☐ ÷ ☐ = ☐
9 × ☐ = ☐ ⟶ ☐ ÷ ☐ = ☐ ⟶ ☐ ÷ ☐ = ☐
9 × ☐ = ☐ ⟶ ☐ ÷ ☐ = ☐ ⟶ ☐ ÷ ☐ = ☐

Finish these multiplication frames.

Date:

×	2	4	3	6	5
6					
8					
7					
10					
9					

×	7	6	5	9	8
6					
10					
8					
9					
7					

×	5							
4	20	40		8			36	
7	35		21		28			
9		90		18		72		
6					36		48	
8			24					56

×								
	63		54		72		90	
		63		35		14		21
	42		36				60	
		72		40		16		32
	70		60		80			

31

100 Square.

Date:

1. Place a cross in the top left hand corner of each number which can be divided exactly by 6 ⟶

1	2	3	4	5	ˣ6	7△	8₀	9▫	10
11	ˣ12	13	14△	15	16₀	17	ˣ18▫	19	20
21	22	23	24	25	26	27	28	29	30
31	32	33	34	35	36	37	38	39	40
41	42	43	44	45	46	47	48	49	50
51	52	53	54	55	56	57	58	59	60
61	62	63	64	65	66	67	68	69	70
71	72	73	74	75	76	77	78	79	80
81	82	83	84	85	86	87	88	89	90
91	92	93	94	95	96	97	98	99	100

2. Draw a triangle in the top right hand corner of each number which can be divided by 7.

3. Place a circle in the bottom left hand corner of each number which can be divided by 8.

4. Draw a square in the bottom right hand corner of each number which can be divided by 9.

32

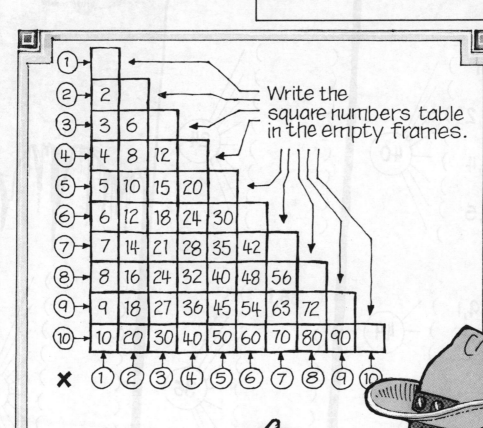

Finish these mappings.   Date:

(20, 1)
(1, 20)
(10, 2)
(   ) → 20
(5, 4)
(   )

(40, 1)
(20, 2)
(   )
(10, 4) → 40
(   )
(8, 5)
(   )

(49, 1)
(   ) → 49
(   )

(32, 1)
(   )
(   ) → 32
(   )
(   )
(   )

(12, 1)
(   )
(   ) → 12
(   )
(   )

(   )
(   )
(   ) → 24
(   )
(   )
(   )

(36, 1)
(   )
(   )
(   ) → 36
(   )
(   )

(   )
(   )
(   ) → 48
(   )
(   )

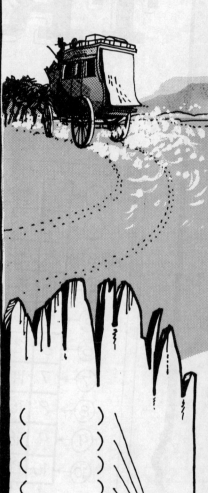

Multiplication pairs.

Date:

Using multiplication pairs, we can obtain 1 as a product like this:

[1]
1 × 1

We can obtain 2 as a product like this:

[2]
2 × 1
or
1 × 2

We can obtain 4 as a product like this:

[3]
4 × 1
1 × 4
2 × 2

Show all the ways we can obtain :−

[6]
6 × 1
1 × 6
3 × 2
2 × 3

[8]

[9]

[10]

[12]

[14]

[15]

[16]

[18]

[20]

[21]

[11]

[25]

[27]

[30]

[31]

[48]

[49]

[50]

[60]

[100]

35

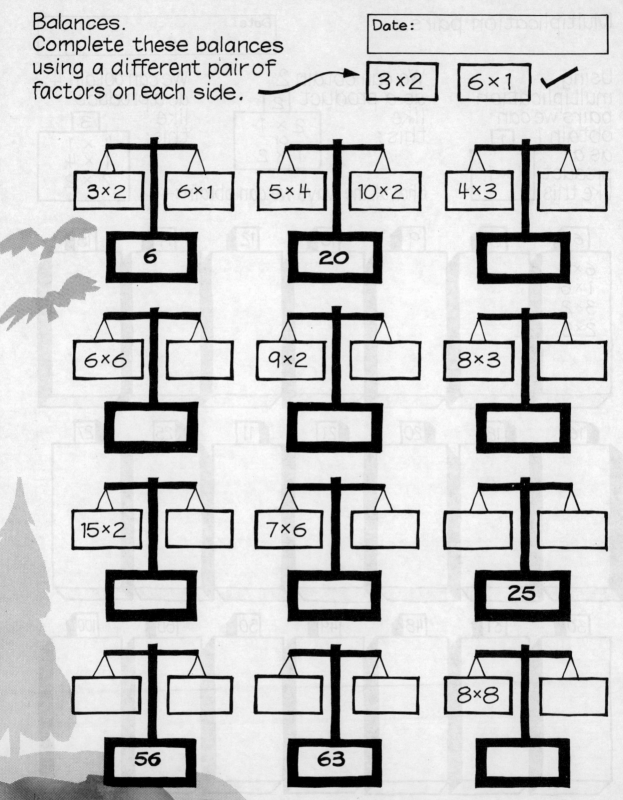

Date:

5×4 can be written
5+5+5+5.
Both equal 20.

Finish these:

5×3 →	5+5+5 →	15
4×2 →	→	8
3×6 →	→	
☐ →	7+7+7+7 →	
9×4 →	→	
☐ →	8+8+8+8+8 →	
7×8 →	→	
8×7 →	→	
☐ →	→	63
☐ →	→	42

Now make up four of your own examples.

37

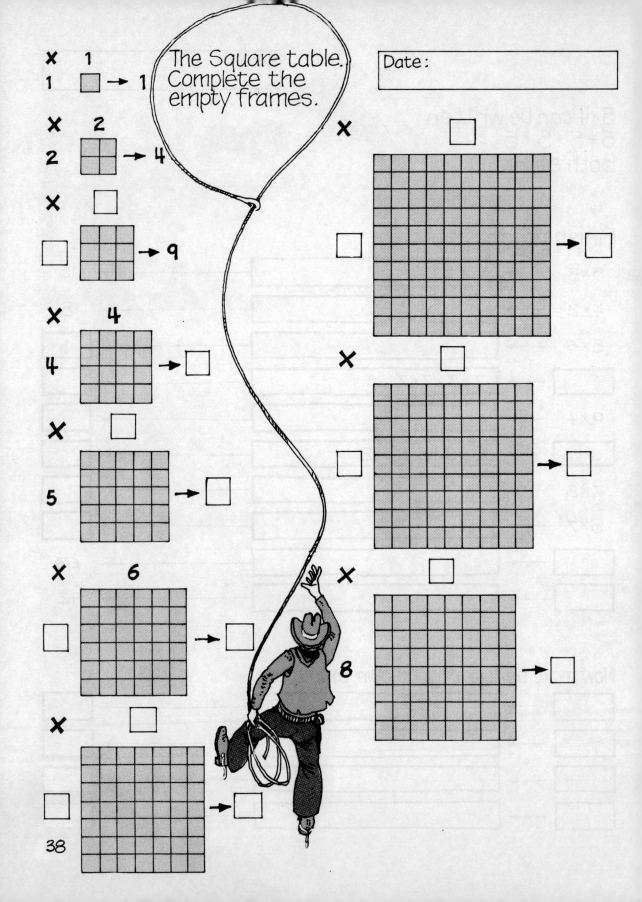

Dividing and multiplying are connected.

Date:

$6 \div 3 = 2$ $2 \times 3 = 6$

Complete these:

$20 \div 10 =$ ☐	$20 \div 5 =$ ☐
$70 \div 10 =$ ☐	$25 \div 5 =$ ☐
$100 \div 10 =$ ☐	$35 \div 5 =$ ☐
$20 \div 2 =$ ☐	$12 \div 6 =$ ☐
$12 \div 2 =$ ☐	$42 \div 6 =$ ☐
$18 \div 2 =$ ☐	$60 \div 6 =$ ☐
$9 \div 3 =$ ☐	$32 \div 8 =$ ☐
$15 \div 3 =$ ☐	$56 \div 8 =$ ☐
$27 \div 3 =$ ☐	$64 \div 8 =$ ☐
$12 \div 4 =$ ☐	$9 \div 9 =$ ☐
$24 \div 4 =$ ☐	$45 \div 9 =$ ☐
$36 \div 4 =$ ☐	$63 \div 9 =$ ☐

Write out the table for dividing by 7..

$7 \div 7 = 1$	☐ $\div 7 =$ ☐
$14 \div 7 = 2$	☐ $\div 7 =$ ☐
$\boxed{21} \div 7 =$ ☐	☐ $\div 7 =$ ☐
☐ $\div 7 =$ ☐	☐ $\div 7 =$ ☐
☐ $\div 7 =$ ☐	☐ $\div 7 =$ ☐

Try to find a connection between multiplication and division.

MAKE A Tables Tower

You need —
2 plastic containers (of slightly different diameters), scouring pads, powder, knife, scissors, fibre-tipped pen.

1. Cut the tops and bottoms off the two containers.

cut here

2. Clean off the print using scouring pads and powder.

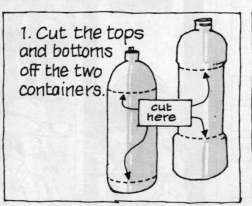

3. Cut a 'window' of about 1cm² half way up the larger container.

4. Write the numbers 1–10 (equally spaced) around the bottom of the larger container.

Use a fibre-tipped pen.

Ask for help in making your Tables Tower – especially **with the cutting-out stages** 1 and 2 and with stages 4 and 5. Try to do the rest yourself.

40

5. Write the numbers 1-10 on the lower half of the smaller container as shown.

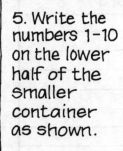
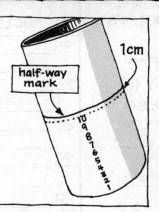

6. Insert the smaller container into the larger.

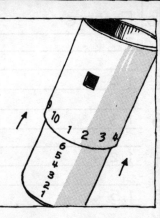

7. Line up the numbers on the two containers (barrel slide rule principle) and write the products in the window.

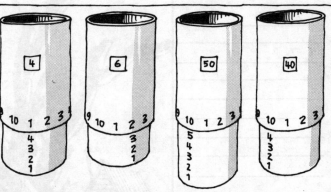

8. View of completed smaller container.

You can use your Tables Tower for tables practice.

Factors.

4 can be divided exactly by 1, 2 and 4. These are called the factors of 4.

The factors of 10 are 1, 2, 5 and 10. Complete these factors charts. (Try to write each set of factors in order, smallest first).

No.	Factors
1	1
2	1, 2
3	1, 3
4	1, 2, 4
5	1, 5
6	1, 2, 3, 6
7	1, 7
8	
9	
10	
11	
12	
13	
14	
15	
16	
17	
18	
19	

No.	Factors
20	
21	
22	
23	
24	

No.	Factors
25	
26	
27	
28	
29	
30	
31	
32	
33	
34	
35	
36	
37	
38	
39	
40	
41	
42	
43	

Date: _____

No.	Factors
44	
45	
46	
47	
48	
49	
50	
51	
52	
53	
54	
55	
56	
57	
58	
59	
60	
61	
62	

No.	Factors
63	
64	
65	
66	
67	
68	
69	
70	
71	
72	
73	
74	
75	
76	
77	
78	
79	
80	
81	

No.	Factors
82	
83	
84	
85	
86	
87	
88	
89	
90	
91	
92	
93	
94	
95	
96	
97	
98	
99	
100	

More connections.

Date:

6 appears as a product in the 2, the 3, and the 6 tables.

Find some other products which appear in three or more tables. Use the chart for your recording.

Product	Appears in these tables
6	1 2 3 6
30	1 2 3 5 6 10 15 30
24	1 2 3 ☐ ☐ ☐ ☐ ☐
50	1 2 ☐ ☐ ☐ ☐
42	1 ☐ ☐ ☐ ☐ ☐ ☐

Connections.
Fill in the blank circles.

Date:

| Double the products for the two table and you have the products for the four table. | 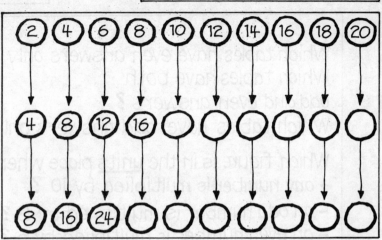 |
| Double the products for the four table and you have the products for the eight table. | |

| Double the products for the three table and you have the products for the six table | 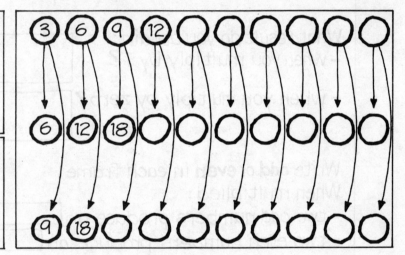 |
| Treble the products for the three table and you have the products for the nine table. | |

| Double the products for the five table and you have the products for the ten table. | 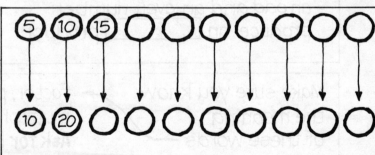 |

45

Question time.

Date:

Which tables have even answers only ? ⬜
Which tables have both
odd and even answers ? ⬜
Which tables have odd answers only ? ⬜

Which figure is in the <u>units</u> place when :
- any number is multiplied by 10 ? ⬜
- an odd number is multiplied by 5 ? ⬜
- an even number is multiplied by 5 ? ⬜

What result do you obtain :
- when you multiply by 1 ? ⬜

- when you multiply by zero ? ⬜

Write **odd** or **even** in each frame.
When multiplied:
- two odd numbers produce an ⬜ product.
- two even numbers produce an ⬜ product.
- an odd and an even number
  produce an ⬜ product.

Make sure you know ➝ factor, product, multiplier,
the meaning   multiplicand.
of these words ⟵ **Ask for help if necessary.**

46

Hands up!
-for the finger calculator.

Date:

Number your finger-nails from 6-10 starting from the thumbs. (You will need a felt-pen and a friend).

To find the product of 8 and 7, place the 8 finger of one hand against the 7 finger of the other, palms downward.

1.
Count the fingers nearest to you and include the touching fingers.

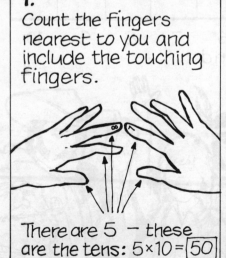

There are 5 — these are the tens: 5×10 = 50

2.
Multiply the numbers of remaining fingers on each hand.
2 × 3 = 6

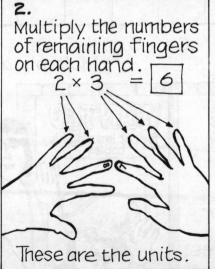

These are the units.

3.
Add the two parts.

50+6 = 56

so: 8×7 = 56

Try this with your friends!

Tables record.

Date:

Multiplier										
10										
9										
8										
7										
6										
5										
4										
3										
2										
1										
X	1	2	3	4	5	6	7	8	9	10

Multiplicand

The tables facts which you know are to be recorded on this chart. Instructions for recording are given in the notes.
WANTED
for not knowing his tables